The Italian Professor's Wife

Also by Ann Pedone

POETRY
The Medea Notebooks

CHAPBOOKS
Sea [break]
perhaps there is a sky we don't know: a re-imagining of sappho
Everywhere You Put Your Mouth
DREAM/WORK
The Bird Happened

The Italian Professor's Wife

Winner of the 2022 Press 53 Award for Poetry

Ann Pedone

Press 53

Winston-Salem

Press 53, LLC
PO Box 30314
Winston-Salem, NC 27130

The Italian Professor's Wife

Winner of the 2022 Press 53 Award for Poetry

First Edition

A Tom Lombardo Poetry Selection

Cover design by Claire V. Foxx, Kevin Morgan Watson, and Ann Pedone

Library of Congress Control Number
2022932796

Printed on acid-free paper
ISBN 978-1-950413-42-3

Acknowledgments

Thank you to the editors of the following journals for publishing earlier versions of these poems: *Streetcake Magazine*, *San Antonio Review*, *Menacing Hedge*, *Permafrost*, *Drunk Monkeys*, and *Juked*.

This book would not have been possible without the love, support, and patience of my children. I also want to express my deep gratitude to my friends—both new and old—for their conversation, guidance, and inspiration.

"Marriage is memory, marriage is time.
Marriage is not only time: it is also,
paradoxically, the denial of time."

— Joan Didion

The Italian Professor's Wife

Jan. 13, 1997

Spent the afternoon
looking up flights to Italy
Rome and then Bologna
might rent a car at that point
and head further north
he said something last night about
wanting to be in Verona by late spring

The airport closest
to the Colosseum is the Ciampino
13 km away
I made a note of that on an old receipt I found
in my sweater pocket then the
computer went dead and I fell asleep.

Jan. 17th

Church bells at 11
three police sirens
9, 10:30, the last
not more than
fifteen minutes ago

The Financial Times
three Italian papers
left in the hallway

Stripped the bed found
the train tickets tried
calling my sister picked up
his pants from
the bathroom floor reached
into the front left
pocket and while he
wasn't looking
held my breath and pulled
the lining all
the way out.

Jan. 19th

Lunch with Ted and Rosemary
up for the
week from Athens

Place we found a couple of years ago
not too far from
the Spanish Steps

The woman at the
next table asked Rosemary how
to say *edicola* in French

He signaled to the waiter twice

Cameriere, posso

While they argued over desert
I reached my left
hand under the table

Subito

Did you see in the paper this morning
something about
sea levels rising in Venice

Sì, telefono domani

He lifted his hand to brush a hair away
from his forehead

No, impossible. Stasera non ho molto tempo

And I held his glass firm between my legs

Perché? Sì, tutti sono gentili

Fiction forms what lives in us she said and
he said, and yes, said the wife

Sì, sì, in greco è gallo

He leaned across the table and
pulled the cigarette out of Ted's mouth

*Non conosco. In italia tutte le donne si
arrampicano sulle pareti. Non hai
letto dante?*

He paid the bill and language
burrowed itself between my legs
in the way Homer says only the gods can

*Caro, caro, a domani
perfetto*

I never asked
to be a husband's last story

Vieni qui.

It is January and I am in the wrong city
speaking the wrong language

Jan. 22nd

Thirty minutes getting
directions to the
Egyptian Museum
we ended up taking a cab

Ran into an old student
outside the
third floor bathrooms
and decided to walk back in the
rain my hair

Was still wet when he tried
to fuck me up
against the bathroom door
only the
maid knew he couldn't
cum until I had
floated up to the ceiling.

Jan. 24th

Rearranged the
carry-ons
called up for more towels

Then the tub
overflowed and that
constant click
of his tongue
the one that is
all the years of my life.

Jan. 25th

Three days in Florence
and I have yet to make it
across the Arno

Desire comes from the body
the way that tall
woman came into the
lobby last night and
asked for Gigi

He's always the first to point out I speak
Italian with the wrong accent.

Jan. 26th

Did you remember to call the airline?
What the eye refuses to see
You know, this has never been my game
Penelope asleep at the wheel
No. The tickets aren't there. They're in the small blue one
As if a wife existed outside of
language outside of time
Three, four days at the most
No. Non posso, vorrei domani
Sì, lui non è italiano

It was the sound of his writing that woke me.

The Italian Professor's Wife
(The Continuity Script)

SCENE I

A small hotel in Rome

The wife arrives in the lobby

The wife goes up the elevator

The wife unlocks the door and
goes into the room

We hear people in the hallway speaking
Italian with an American accent

Camera pans to the right
follows the wife into the room

The wife sits on a low metal chair, folds
a small piece of paper into thirds

Pushes it into her mouth,
leans her head back, and swallows.

Jan. 27th

Called down to the front desk
Picked up the keys
Dropped off the mail
His lies, I should add, have always been very poetic
Drinks down at the bar
As if it had only happened thirty minutes ago
Wait, I'm trying to remember
His face like Homer in winter
There might have been
Just know, I'll never care what happens to her.

SCENE II

We see the wife at the window

The wife has just gotten out of the shower

We see her in a pale blue dress

We see her hands deep in her pockets

There is a knock at the door

The wife goes over to the door, but does not open it.

Jan. 28th

Florence shook, and I fell back to sleep

from beneath the sheets, nipple to hip

I listened for the signal

earthquake in Istanbul

gas prices higher in France

three letters from the university

one from my sister

2 AM call from his editor

that mix-up with the keys

twenty minutes on my knees last night

while he sat perfectly

straight on the edge of the tub

the next morning he got up early

again the pathos of my left hand

Now I realize

I'm going to have to keep a record of everything

SCENE III

The husband is standing outside

of a small restaurant

He is alone

It has just started to rain

He stands in front of a small table

He looks up at the sky for as long as he can.

Feb. 1st

Sooner or later I will lie down in this room

an animal with its behind high up in the air

and beg for him to enter me (or in other words)

we've never been in love, and that is our beauty.

Feb. 2nd

He's never been a rescuer, his heart
rate has always been too fast

My friends still ask how we got to talking that
summer on Long Island

I lifted the small metal latch
on the bathroom door
and could see that there was
something living between
the tub and the wall

Got down on my hands and knees
and pulled the rim until the wall
cracked open
grabbed a towel from under the
sink and waited.

SCENE IV

The mistress has returned to her room

The camera stays on the empty chair
near the window

She does not sit on the chair.

Feb. 4th

Had a one o'clock
train to catch, so decided to
grab a quick lunch at a place
he knew of behind the basilica

Couple next to us speaking Greek
with an accent I couldn't place

The man moved his left hand onto his lap

She opened her blouse to the fourth button

Three plates of olives on the table
what looked like a bowl of anchovies and
two ashtrays

No, next time I want you to watch me when I do it.

SCENE V

A small table at the hotel bar

He is checking his watch

Did you tell her?

Yes

Are you telling me the truth?

Why would I lie?

Same reason why you would tell me the truth.

Feb. 6th

Looked down and saw
the spot on the bed had
grown wider and thick

When he
turned the
water off I
leaned down and
sucked it up as far
into my mouth as
I could.

SCENE VI

The wife is seated on the edge of the bed

The husband is pacing back and forth

The wife looks out the window

The wife unbuttons her blouse

The husband looks out the window

The wife takes her blouse off

The husband opens the desk drawer

The wife pulls her skirt down to her ankles

The husband pulls out an envelope

The wife takes it out of his hand and

Places it on the table.

Feb. 19th

He had gone out to
find the American
Express office and I
went down to the lobby
not for the sake
of sex, but for language.

SCENE VII

The wife goes into the bathroom

The wife turns on the light

The wife looks at herself in the mirror

She hears a pigeon settle on the balcony railing

She touches her finger to her lips twice

She turns off the light.

Feb. 20th

Bill called

Did you see the email?

No, lunedi, sabato
Mi ha chiesto di
essere in Napoli il
prima possibile

I heard nothing and paid the check.

SCENE VIII

The mistress moves away from the window

We hear the sound of running water

Large chairs being dragged across
the floor

Church bells in the distance

The mistress turns off the lights
and lies down on the left side of the bed

The mistress swallows.

Feb. 25th

This morning there were
goats in the bathtub and no one
knows where they came from

Orange is a slow color, although not as
slow as black

Kafka steps off the bridge
falls into the Vltava
papers in the air like flames

We must have been very lonely
people to have done this to each other.

Feb. 29th

The maid left a stack of new towels on
top of the TV

Three Turkish men have been arguing
in the hallway since lunch

While I was brushing my teeth this morning
he came out of the shower and
wrote something
on the bathroom mirror

I left the door unlocked when
we got into bed

And drained all the
milk from between my thighs.

SCENE IX

We see the wife going down in the elevator

We see the wife sit at a small table in the hotel bar

We see the wife order a glass of wine

We see the wife look down to the end of the bar

The husband is sitting next to a woman

The wife watches them

Light fills all of the openings in the room

The wife can see that the woman is beautiful.

March 1st

Every night the lobby fills with
women who hold their hands
firm on their hips

Pink prints on white walls

Cavafy in the second elevator
smoking a cigarette

This morning I gathered
all of the letters of his name
and dropped them in the bathtub

I want to make a cup of coffee

I want a piece of cake.

March 3rd

The canal is fogged
my lips muddied (6 AM)

The maid comes in with fresh towels
Perché la tua faccia è
sulla tua testa? (9:30 AM)

Fall asleep and dream I am at my
mother's in New Hampshire

She's painted the inside of the house blue
the walls, chairs, floors, everything was blue
(12 PM)

The phone hasn't rung all day and
this is all I will remember.
(1:30 PM)

March 5th

To desire
Is to remain uncut
(he will never understand)

All light derives from the
Western window

Remember that.

SCENE X

The husband is standing outside of a small restaurant

The streets are soaked with rain

He sits down at a table

Takes out a book

Lights a cigarette and waits.

March 10th

In this city: none of the girls are allowed outside

E' tutto finito

Reason produces sleep: but sleep produces no reason

This morning I heard the women
in the market say
that during the Middle Ages
the priests here would burn coffee
to conceal the smell of death

but I am deathless

My husband is sitting
on the floor: cross-
legged like a school girl

I lay in bed eating fat
rendered from the dead
my body warm
under the sheets

This is Venice: a city
that follows the rules
of misdirection: a woman
whose holes have all
filled with water.

SCENE XI

The interior of the American
Express office

The room is large and dark

The husband approaches one
of the clerks seated behind a long
marble counter

The husband tells the clerk he wants
to cash three traveler's checks

Just as the clerk takes out his ledger,
the husband suddenly turns his back to him

Track follows as he walks out
of the office and onto the street

The husband takes a few steps forward

The clerk comes out of the office

From the inside of the office, we see
the clerk call after the husband

The husband does not turn around

The husband takes off his coat

The husband takes off his shoes

The husband looks up at the sky
and opens his mouth twice.

March 20th

I sent out the dry cleaning four days ago

The three stray dogs outside the window

$1,350 worth of traveler's checks in my bag

My passport expires in two years

Before we left, my sister insisted that I pack
three pairs of shoes, but I see now that two
would have been enough.

April 1st

Behind the elevator
right over there
he took him out of her mouth
made the sign of the cross
and sent him back to bed
(Or at least, this is what I was told)

SCENE XII

The wife is sitting alone at a cafe

She looks out at the piazza in front of her

A group of nuns walks in front of the camera

The mistress lights a cigarette

The wife tucks her hair behind her ears

The mistress picks up her bag

The wife looks up at the sky

The wife opens her mouth twice.

April 15th

Woke up cold under the sheets

And slid my left
index finger
as far into
his mouth as
I could.

May 1st

Or: what makes the body cum?
What makes us fall in love?
Brass door pulls, medieval
city walls, small silver
pitchers of cream,
a tall, lean man exposing himself
in front of a fountain

Or: what do we fear?
Not having something to
hold onto at dusk?
The return of a long-lost father?

Last night I woke up in the hotel basement
Crawfish scuttled across my chest
My hands purple with dream
We dared each other to see
who would push off the pier first

Once my husband told me that
he loved me because he was good at it

There are two kinds of people in this world
Those who eat salt
And those who wait for a perfect ending.

SCENE XIV

The husband and the mistress
down at the hotel bar

Do you think she heard you

He looks at his watch

If we could just get away. Just the two of us

He looks at his watch.

SCENE XV

The husband is standing at the bathroom sink shaving

The wife is standing in the doorway

The wife is wearing a white silk blouse

The wife begins to unbutton it

The wife sees her lipstick on the edge of the sink

The wife picks up the lipstick and draws two large red circles around her nipples

The wife reddens her nipples

The wife smears the lipstick on her chest,
her belly, her thighs

The husband turns off the sink, steps past his wife,
and goes back into the bedroom.

May 20th

He has been wading in the river

Each forward movement

I bend at the hip

Because a boy once forced
himself into my mouth

I want to say, he inhabited

And my husband

I could describe the symptoms to you over dinner

I have always enjoyed the taste of hunger

But never as a metaphor.

SCENE XVI

The wife is sitting alone in a hotel room

The wife sits lower on her hips,
relaxes her weight into the chair

The wife lets her legs fall open,
and reaches her hand down

The telephone rings.

May 25th

A marriage is
nothing unusual

The smooth cold from
his mouth to mine

Into nothing
one

Takes an idea

Knows it is outside
of time

The body splits
itself perpetually

I would have loved
to have argued

Click

End of scene.

SCENE XVII

Santa Lucia Railway Station
Early Evening

We see the wife standing in line at the ticket counter

Her hair is piled up on the top of her head

We see her walk through the station

She is wearing a long navy blue dress with a white belt

The train for Palermo leaves at 6:12.

Ann Pedone is the author of *The Medea Notebooks*, and the chapooks *The Bird Happened*; *perhaps there is a sky we don't know: a re-imagining of sappho*; DREAM/WORK; *Everywhere You Put Your Mouth*; and *Sea [Break]*. She lives in the San Francisco Bay Area.

www.ingramcontent.com/pod-product-compliance
Lightning Source LLC
Chambersburg PA
CBHW031806090426
42739CB00008B/1180